REJOICE, MARY

GIANCARLO BRUNI

REJOICE, MARY

LECTIO DIVINA OF THE HAIL MARY

St Paul Publications

Original title: *Rallegrati, Maria. "Lectio divina" sull'Ave Maria.*
© Figlie San Paolo, Milano, Italy 1987.

Translated from the Italian by Paul McPartlan

Scripture quotations are from the Jerusalem Bible, published and copyright 1966, 1967 and 1968 by Darton, Longman and Todd Ltd and Doubleday & Co Inc, and are used by permission of the publishers.
Quotations from the Psalms: (c) The Grail (England) 1963.

Cover design: *Icon of the Annunciation* by M. Lee
      (St Charles Borromeo, Ogle Street, London)
Graphics by Mary Lou Winters, fsp

St Paul Publications
Middlegreen, Slough SL3 6BT, England

English translation copyright
© St Paul Publications 1988

Typeset by Society of St Paul, Slough
Printed by Hollen Street Press, Slough
ISBN 085439 278 5

St Paul Publications is an activity of the priests and brothers of the Society of St Paul who proclaim the Gospel through the media of social communication

CONTENTS

PREFACE	7
THE HAIL MARY	9
Praise	
Petition	
Lectio Divina	
MARY, MODEL OF *LECTIO DIVINA*	18
A presence	
A presence of listening put into practice	
A presence of listening pondered, sung and announced	
REJOICE, MARY	24
From *Hail* to the *Magnificat*	
Our joy	
FULL OF GRACE	31
The Graced One	
Mary and Israel	
The graced ones	
THE LORD IS WITH YOU	38
History of vocations	
Vocation and the Spirit	
BLESSED AMONG WOMEN	46
Blessing-Benediction	
She who is blessed	
We who are blessed	

BLESSED IS THE FRUIT OF YOUR WOMB, JESUS ... 53
    She is blessed in view of the Blessed One
    Jesus
    At the heart of the *Hail Mary*

HOLY MARY ... 58
    From her who is holy to the 'thrice Holy'
    Far off
    Near to sanctify
    Holy Mary

MOTHER OF GOD ... 64
    Theotòkos
    Wonderful exchange
    Mother and image of the Church

PRAY FOR US SINNERS ... 71
    The great intercessor
    The Church, the Body of Christ who intercedes
    Tenderness turned into intercession

NOW AND AT THE HOUR OF DEATH – AMEN ... 77
    Today and the hour
    Amen

CONCLUSION ... 83

THE STRUCTURE OF
    PERSONAL *LECTIO DIVINA* ... 84
    Preliminaries
    Structure

INDEX OF BIBLICAL REFERENCES ... 91
    Old Testament
    New Testament

PREFACE

The term *Lectio Divina* means reading of the sacred or divine Scriptures done in the company of the Holy Spirit and in the communion of saints. Therefore, reading the Hail Mary in this perspective is acknowledging its scriptural character.

Doing so is absolutely correct. Its praise is composed of explicit biblical references and, even though not in a strictly literal sense, its petition is saturated with scriptural recollection, so much so that the full extent of its meaning can be brought to light only by pondering it in the light of the Word.

With thankfulness for the gift of this woman, the image of what the Church and the whole creation are called to become, the *lectio* which follows is nothing other than an unpretentious attempt to understand more deeply the meaning of the words:

Hail,
full of grace,
the Lord is with you.
You are blessed among all women

and blessed is the fruit of your
womb.
Holy Mary,
Mother of God,
pray for us sinners,
now and at the hour of our death.
Amen.

THE HAIL MARY

The *Hail Mary* consists of two parts, one of praise and the other of petition.

Praise

Our praise, which fulfils what was foretold in the *Magnificat* canticle: 'from now onwards all generations will call me blessed', is made up from the words addressed to Mary by the angel Gabriel (Lk 1:28) and by Elizabeth (Lk 1:42).

Rejoice,
you who enjoy God's favour!
The Lord is with you.
Of all women you are the most blessed
and blessed is the fruit of your womb.

It follows that:

1. Among the praises of Mary none equals this, because of its objectively revealed and eminently biblical character. It is the norm

given and received, against which all other praise must be measured.

2. This praise introduces whoever proclaims it into a long, uninterrupted line of prayer which, beginning ideally with Gabriel and Elizabeth, is charged with the voice of the centuries and reaches down to our days, continuing in us.

The witness of Theodore of Ancyra comes from the first half of the fifth century: 'Urged on by the opening words of the angel, let us say: Hail, full of grace, the Lord is with you'.

The greeting of the angel and the blessing of Elizabeth begin to appear together in a Syriac baptismal liturgy of the sixth century and in the Eastern liturgies of St James (in the Jerusalem Church), St Mark (in the Coptic Church) and St John Chrysostom (in the Church of Constantinople). Then finally there was the discovery in Egypt, at Luxor, of a clay fragment, presumably from the seventh century, with the text: 'Hail Mary, full of grace, the Lord is with you, blessed are you among all women and blessed is the fruit of your womb, because you conceived Christ, the Son of God, the Redeemer of our souls'. This confirms the existence of a longstanding tradition of prayer which in the West was already foreshadowed in Leo the Great and was to find full written formulation in the *De laudibus Virginis* (The Praises of the Virgin) of Amadeus of Lausanne, a disciple of Bernard, in the twelfth century.

In the thirteenth century this prayer was adopted by the Cistercians, the Premonstratensians, the Dominicans and the Servants of Saint Mary and at the same time it started to be explained to the people.

3. Founded on the Bible and recited in communion with the Church of all places and all times and with the angelic world itself, represented by Gabriel, the *Hail Mary* is possible only as a 'Pneumatological' event, as an exclamation in the Spirit: 'Elizabeth was filled with the Holy Spirit. She gave a loud cry and said, "blessed..., blessed..."' (Lk 1:41-42:45).

In Elizabeth there is understood each believer. Just as no one can say 'Our Father' except in the Spirit, so 'Hail' or 'Blessed' cannot be said except in the same Spirit.

Though recited in the Spirit and in the communion of saints, the *Hail Mary* in no way competes with or gives grounds for dimming the singular praise owed to the Father. What is celebrated in Mary is the omnipotent mercy of God who has done great things in her (Lk 1:49); within the praise of the Virgin lies the praise of her Creator, whom Mary herself glorifies with the Church of all times in prayer (Ac 1:14).

Petition

The invocation used in litanies, 'Holy Mary, pray for us', eventually gave origin to the second part of the *Hail Mary*. Before attaining its present form this underwent, from the fourteenth century onwards, varying phases and formulations within different contexts: in Italy, Germany, Belgium and Holland, England, France...

Towards the middle of the fourteenth century we find, for example, the Servants of Saint Mary of Florence using the following formula:

Ave,
dulcissima et immaculata
   Virgo Maria,
benedicta tu in mulieribus
et benedictus fructus ventris tui
   Iesus.
Sancta Maria, Mater Dei,
mater gratiae et misericordiae,
ora pro nobis
   nunc et in hora mortis.
Amen.

Hail,
most sweet and immaculate
Virgin Mary,
you are blessed among women
and blessed is the fruit of your womb,
Jesus.
Holy Mary, Mother of God,
mother of grace and mercy,
pray for us now
and at the hour of death. Amen.

While underlining the rather unique expression 'mother of grace and mercy', it is also worth mentioning the addition of the name 'Jesus' at the end of the first part of the *Hail Mary*. Its origin is attributed to Urban IV (1261-1264). The 'now and at the hour of death', first found in a Carthusian breviary of 1350, was taken up again in the Franciscan breviary of 1525.

On the other hand, the term 'sinners', which we find in the fourteenth century Carthusian breviary referred to, does not appear elsewhere. Very often the expression became the object of Bernardino of Siena's popular preaching; he used to insist, 'I cannot stop myself from adding: Holy Mary, pray for us sinners'. Soon this was added in the Catechism of Peter Canisius, which indicates the recitation of the second part of the Hail Mary as follows: 'Holy Mary, mother of God, pray for us sinners. Amen'.

In 1568, Pius V gathered together the various scattered elements and fixed the formula of petition in the form in which we still use today:

Holy Mary,
Mother of God,
pray for us sinners,
now and at the hour of our death.
Amen.

The Bible supports the legitimacy of having recourse to someone that they might 'pray for us'. Paul asks this for himself and for his closest collaborators from the Thessalonians (2 Th 3:1), the Corinthians (2 Co 1:11), the Romans (Rm 15:30) and the Colossians (Col 4:3) and he himself becomes an intercessor for the Churches founded by him and for Israel (Rm 10:1), urging prayer on a number of occasions for all the 'saints', the name by which the Christians are known (Ep 6:18), and for all people (1 Tm 2:1). The reason is that the Lord turns his ear to the prayer of the just (1 Pt 3:12). Such prayer has great power (Jm 5:16) and rises to God with the smoke of the incense (Rv 8:4) and with the alms of the charitable (Ac 10:4).

Rooted in its original experience of prayer

one for another (Jm 5:16), the praying Church in all times and places does not fear, as is clear from the Roman eucharistic Canon and Eucharistic Prayer III, to turn to its saints, 'on whose constant intercession we rely' and among whom 'Mary, the virgin Mother of God' is foremost, in order to obtain 'blessings and protection' from the Father in the present and at the hour of death.

More precisely, as the Scriptures and the great liturgical tradition indicate, petition is always addressed to the Father through the Son in the Spirit. The community and individuals trustingly dare to entreat the 'saints' of heaven and earth, with whom they are in communion, to unite their supplication for us to the voice of the great intercessor, Jesus Christ (Rm 3:24; Heb 7:25; 1 Jn 2:1). In this light, saying 'Holy Mary, pray for us' means: you who are the woman of prayer in our midst and with us (Ac 1:14), together with your Son, intercede for us with the God of mercies. May this, your intercession for us with the Father, be enduring, each day and at the hour of death.

Lectio Divina

The short commentary which follows is inspired in its main lines by the classical method of *lectio divina*: reading *(lectio)*, reflection *(meditatio),* prayer *(oratio)* and contemplation *(contemplatio).* This is a method which springs from desire *(desideratur)* more than from the longing to ask questions *(quaesitur)* and from experience *(experiendum)* more than from the craving to know *(sciendum).*

Not that the *lectio divina* which is proper to the monastic tradition is to be contrasted radically with the *lectio magistralis* which is proper to the university school. The trilogy of reading *(lectio)*, the questions which it poses *(quaestio)* and the discussion which follows from it *(disputatio)* with the aim of an ever clearer intellectual elucidation of the text, can constitute a useful preliminary to the *lectio divina* itself, in accord with what is written in Acts 8:30: 'Do you understand what you are reading?'

But the ultimate purpose of *lectio* cannot and must not be simply a rational comprehension of the text. However, once this necessary basis has been reached, through the invocation of the Spirit, one asks to be permitted to attain to a wise and heartfelt understanding of it and to a contemplation of the message which will open up one's whole being to praise, to prayer which the reading has inspired and to an existence faithful to the word received, striving to proclaim it with one's voice and life.

Contemplation is never an escape into interiority or into the imaginary or into an absolute void, but a plunging into life in order there daily to witness to what one has been given to hear and to see.

In short, we shall approach the text of the *Hail Mary* following this method of reading and listening for which the Virgin herself is a sure model.

MARY,
MODEL OF *LECTIO DIVINA*

A presence

In John 19:26-27 it is written: 'Seeing his mother and the disciple whom he loved standing near her, Jesus said to his mother, "Woman, this is your son." Then to the disciple he said, "This is your mother." And from that hour the disciple took her into his home.' Since that moment Mary has been part of the gifts which Jesus on the Cross left in the keeping of his Church, a gift present at the start among the brethren praying in Jerusalem (Ac 1:14) and today, as the Roman Canon indicates, in every assembly gathered for the 'thanksgiving'. 'In union with the whole Church we honour Mary, the ever-virgin mother of Jesus Christ our Lord and God...'. Mary thus becomes a presence contemplating which we find, in a limited and illustrative way, a model for placing ourselves before the Lord who is speaking to us.

A presence of listening put into practice

Let us call upon the New Testament witness. 'In the sixth month the angel Gabriel was sent by God to a town in Galilee called Nazareth, to a virgin betrothed to a man named Joseph, of the House of David; and the virgin's name was Mary. He went in and said to her...' (Lk 1:26-28).

'His mother and his brothers came looking for him, but they could not get to him because of the crowd. He was told, "Your mother and brothers are standing outside and want to see you." But he said in answer, "My mother and my brothers are those who hear the word of God and put it into practice"' (Lk 8:19-21).

'It happened that as he was speaking, a woman in the crowd raised her voice and said, "Blessed the womb that bore you and the breasts that fed you!" But he replied, "More blessed still are those who hear the word of God and keep it!"' (Lk 11:27-28).

Mary stands before and within the community of believers as the woman who has listened to what was said and put it into practice, the epitome of Israel, the listening people. This characteristic is underlined, for instance:

– in the credo of Deuteronomy 6:4: 'Listen,

Israel: Yahweh our God is the one, the only Yahweh';

– in the continuous experience of the Servant of Yahweh: 'Morning by morning he makes my ear alert to listen like a disciple. Lord Yahweh has opened my ear and I have not resisted, I have not turned away' (Is 50:4-5);

– in the impassioned song of the poet: 'They are happy whose life is blameless, who follow God's law! They are happy who do his will... I will obey your statutes' (Ps 118[119]:1-2,8).

Mary is also the perfect image of the community of the disciples, of those who are the friends of the Lord because they are rooted in a word which is no longer secret, but which demands to be lived.

'Everyone who comes to me and listens to my word and acts upon them... is like the man who... dug deep, and laid the foundations on rock' (Lk 6:47-48). 'You are my friends, if you do what I command you... I call you friends, because I have made known to you everything I have learnt from my Father' (Jn 15:14-15).

The Virgin of listening-put-into-practice – the first and last act of each *lectio divina* – is given to the churches and to consciences as a living and permanent example of how to stand before the God of Jesus Christ: not besieging him with words in the manner of the pagans (Mt 6:7), but listening to what is said – the portion of the Word in the daily liturgy and the abundant Word on Sunday – which seeks evangelically to orientate the listeners' way of life, as the Virgin herself recalls: 'Do whatever he tells you' (Jn 2:5).

A presence of listening pondered, sung and announced

The Virgin who listens is at the same time the Virgin who keeps and meditates upon the word: 'As for Mary, she treasured all these things [happenings and words] and pondered them in her heart' (Lk 2:19).

She is the Virgin who questions: 'Mary said to the angel, "But how can this come about...?"' (Lk 1:34); 'My child, why have you done this to us?' (Lk 2:48).

She is the Virgin who announces: 'Mary set out at that time and went as quickly as she could into the hill country...' (Lk 1:39-45), clearly a missionary journey, preceding the apostolic travels. Mary brings the word dwelling within her to the devout (Elizabeth) and to the prophets (John the Baptist) of Israel.

She is also, the Virgin who does not understand: 'But they did not understand what he meant' (Lk 2:50; 2:33,48).

The Virgin who praises: 'My soul proclaims the greatness of the Lord and my spirit rejoices in God my Saviour' (Lk 1:46-47).

The Virgin of sorrow: 'and a sword will pierce your soul too' (Lk 2:35); and yet blessed: 'Yes, blessed is she who believed that the promise made her by the Lord would be fulfilled' (Lk 1:45).

The delicate texture of these quotations, which reflect the Virgin Mary's journeying into wisdom in relation to the Word made flesh within her, introduces us to the full understanding of what *lectio divina* is.

It is listening, by means of reading *(lectio)*, to a word received, guarded and pondered in the depths of our own being, the heart *(meditatio-ruminatio)*.

It is, therefore, a wise and nourishing reflection in the spirit, and one not lacking in questions because 'the heavens are as high above earth as my ways are above your ways, my thoughts above your thoughts' (Is 55:9). And it is, nevertheless, able to turn into prayer of praise, of thanksgiving, of intercession for the world *(oratio)* and into proclamation with our lips and with our life of what we have been given to know *(contemplata tradere)*.

And all of this in joy: 'I take delight in your statutes; I will not forget your word... a lamp for my steps and a light for my path' (Ps 118 [119]:16,105). Joy tempered by 'the distress... that God approves' (2 Co 7:9-10), in face of the evidence that the most beautiful Word ever to appear under the sun is subject to the obstacle of not being welcomed and not being recognized (Jn 1:10-11).

Lest such deafness and blindness before the Word of God occur in us, Mary, silent and virgin ground, free from manifold dreams and anxieties and wholly attentive in the Spirit to the Word of God, stands among us as our mother and sister to point out to us the path to follow, so that our *lectio* on the *Hail Mary*, a prayer explicitly made up of biblical words or at least with clear scriptural foundation, may not be in vain.

Free your heart from evil (Mt 13:9), from fickleness (Mt 13:21), from anxiety for worldly things and from the lure of riches (Mt 13:22) which prevent the Word from putting down roots and bearing fruit (Mt 13:23) and beg for the coming of the Holy Spirit, the secret guest who awaits and disposes to await in quiet and peace the seed of the Word.

Let us begin with *Rejoice, Mary*.

REJOICE, MARY

From Rejoice *to the* Magnificat

The first part of the *Hail Mary* centres on praise. The first word of it, which reading and recitation set deep within us, there to be meditated, is an imperative addressed by the angel to Mary. It is a word to Mary: *Chaire* in Greek and *Ave* in its Latin form, but more correctly, following the line of the Greek Fathers, *Gaude*: be glad, exult, rejoice. This is no casual term. Quite beyond the usual, daily greeting in the Greek *(chaire)* and Latin *(ave)* worlds, Gabriel's *rejoice* reveals an echo of the prophetic announcements of salvation to the 'daughter of Zion':

Shout for joy, daughter of Zion,
Israel, shout aloud!
Rejoice, exult with all your heart,
daughter of Jerusalem!...
Yahweh is king among you, Israel...
When that day comes,
the message for Jerusalem will be:
Zion, have no fear,

do not let your hands fall limp.
Yahweh your God is there with you,
the warrior-Saviour. (Zp 3:14-17)

Land, do not be afraid;
be glad, rejoice,
for Yahweh has done great things...
Sons of Zion, be glad,
rejoice in Yahweh your God;
for he has given you autumn rain...
The threshing-floors
will be full of grain...
And you will know that
I am among you in Israel,
I, Yahweh your God, and no one else.
(Jl 2:21ff.)

Rejoice heart and soul,
daughter of Zion!
Shout for joy, daughter of Jerusalem!
Look, your king is approaching,
he is vindicated and victorious,
humble and riding on a donkey
on a colt, the foal of a donkey.
He will banish chariots from Ephraim
and horses from Jerusalem;
the bow of war will be banished.
He will proclaim peace to the nations.
(Zc 9:9-10)

Jerusalem and Israel are urged to open up to joy, to rejoicing, to exultation and jubilation, notwithstanding the hard recollection of exile and the difficulties of reconstruction and normalization, because out of love the Lord comes into their midst as Saviour. This salvation includes everything, from rain to bread, right up to the dreamed of gift of peace, the 'great thing' which the Lord does for the people whom he loves.

The tragic and cruel experience of exile and its aftermath led Israel to grow in the conviction that bread, joy and peace are the fruit of the kingly Presence *(Shekinah)* of the Lord. Hence, as the following extract from Judaic literature testifies, what really matters is to await the just and victorious king, the only one who is able to confer everlastingly the hoped for gifts. There is no other good news, no other gospel:

"But at the moment when
(in Jerusalem) they announce to her:
Look, your king is approaching,
he is vindicated and victorious (Zc 9:9),
she will say: This indeed is a joy,
in accordance with what is written:
Rejoice heart and soul,
daughter of Zion (Zc 9:9);
and as is said also:

Sing, rejoice, daughter of Zion (Zc 2:14).
In that moment she will exclaim:
I exult for joy in Yahweh,
my soul rejoices in my God (Is 61:10).

Into the *rejoice* of the angel to Mary flows the entire, long line of announcements of salvation to the daughter of Zion. Sweepingly and with great spiritual understanding, Luke brings together Jerusalem and Mary, seeing in the latter the embodiment and the personification of the former.

In the footsteps of Jerusalem, the maiden of Nazareth is called to rejoice because, as the angel announces, the Lord is coming to her, proclaiming that the time has arrived for the fulfilment of the promises of salvation. With the birth (Lk 2:10-11), life (Lk 15:7,9-10) and resurrection (Lk 24:36-52) of the one prophesied and longed for in the heart and on the praying lips of the believing Israel, that is, Christ who is the 'yes' of God to the promises (2 Co 1:19), there begin to be really present the entreated peace, joy and eternal life. Salvation is near for all (Lk 3:6) and because of this work of God the soul of Mary together with the daughter of Zion, whose voice she echoes, glorifies the Lord and her spirit rejoices in God her saviour (Lk 1:46-47).

However, Luke's composition does not

limit itself to specifying the strict link which exists between the daughter of Zion and Mary. It also strives to underline that the former is fulfilled beyond all imagining, in unforeseen superabundance. Thus in Mary there is brought to fulfilment the love of God which confers grace by purifying, by being present and by giving life to sterile wombs.

In illustration:

– she is the Jerusalem and the Israel without blemish of which the Song of Songs speaks (Sg 4:7);

– she has with her and in her the Father, the Son and the Spirit;

– she is the virgin womb from which, by the power of the Spirit, there is born the one awaited, who is more than the Messiah (Lk 1:32) because he is the very Son of God (Lk 1:35), a Saviour to all.

In that *rejoice* our eyes are opened to understand Mary as a unique creature who brings together in herself the daughter of Zion and the oracles linked to her, fulfilling them beyond measure; the virgin loved and constituted without blemish, in a singular way, in order to conceive the Messiah-Son of God, our peace. This is a great mystery before which she who has the Spirit in her exults with intense joy, breaking forth into a song of praise to her Lord and God (Lk 1:46ff.), giving voice to the age-long expectation of Israel and, by extension, to that of every people and nation in the search for its own saviour.

Our joy

This exegesis, by uniting the *rejoice* with the prophetic announcements of the salvation of the daughter of Zion in the Old Testament, on one hand has underlined how no genuine joy is granted unless the Lord is 'in the midst' as the one, true Saviour. On the other hand it has made us understand how the virgin Mary must be read in the light of those same passages, strictly in relation to the jubilation of the holy city and of Israel.

With this understanding which is the work of the Spirit, the master of truth abiding within us, we cannot do other than bursting into a song, together with the same Spirit who prays in us and for us, full of gratitude to the Father for the gift of the Son from the Virgin daughter of Zion, who herself was proclaimed blessed and happy by Elizabeth (Lk 1:42,45) and is so proclaimed in the communion of saints by every generation (Lk 1:48).

Finally, the Spirit makes us begin to see in that woman who was asked to *rejoice*, the purest image of what the Church and every creature are called to be and to become.

Like her, we are chosen for joy and for the knowledge that the source of our blessedness lies in being *flesh* and being *graced* by a God present at our side and in our heart. And, in the Spirit, He asks us to 'generate' the eternal Word for the world by means of the wisdom of our words, holiness of life, transparency of conduct and, even the blood of martyrdom.

Contemplation always leads to praise *(contemplata magnificare)*, to proclamation *(contemplata tradere)* and to new ways of life *(contemplata vivere)*.

FULL OF GRACE

The Graced One

Now, the same messenger, Gabriel, who greeted her and exhorted her to 'rejoice' (*chaire*) for the coming to her of the saviour-God in power in order to beget in her the 'glory' of Israel and the 'light' of the nations (Lk 2:32), completes the salutation calling her *kecharitomene*, 'graced'. *Gratia plena* is how it was unfelicitously rendered by the Vulgate (the Latin translation of the sacred Scripture, produced by St Jerome in the fourth century).

Such a translation in fact suggests the idea of a status, of a Mary brimming with holiness within herself. However, while not denying such a view, as we shall see, this is not the first intention of the evangelist; had it been so he would have used the expression *pleres charitos, full of grace,* which we find in reference to Stephen in Acts 6:8. By using the verb 'bestowing grace upon...with joy' (*charitoo*), Luke wants first and foremost to underline the action of God, who inclines favourably and with joy towards Mary, thereby rendering her a lovable and graceful person in his sight.

Therefore, the translation of '*chaire kecharitomene*' (*Ave, gratia plena*) could be: 'Rejoice, grace has been bestowed upon you', or 'Rejoice, O graced one'. This version highlights both the source of the gift – the grace of the Lord which is at once merciful, generous, faithful, loving and just – and its effect: to render pleasing the person on whom the unconstrained and radically free will of the Lord has decided to bestow grace through a friendly visit.

As Luke explains, this is a decision made in view of the divine motherhood. 'Mary, do not be afraid; you have won God's favour. Look! You are to conceive in your womb and bear a son...' (Lk 1:30-31). On the one hand, these verses give the proper explanation of the 'full of grace' version of Luke 1:28 and on the other, the reason for which it is offered.

This therefore is the immediate and obvious meaning of the term which, however, contemplative *meditatio* must round out by placing it in the wider context of the praying Church's 'pondering' of Mary, a pondering in wisdom.

The one favoured by love, the one who is rendered an absolutely graceful creature before the Father in view of the Son, she is this precisely through being pervaded to the depths of her being by the grace of the sanctifying Spirit, who has constituted her fully holy and wholly beautiful. She is the bright dawn from whom will be born the sun of justice and the uncontaminated root from which will spring the awaited tree of life. She is the full image of the Israel which has been graced and the first-fruits of the Church.

Mary and Israel

The love which determined the choice of Mary, a humble woman from an insignificant village in Galilee, is the same love which determined the choice of Israel.

This latter was a quite gratuitous call, not based on merit, or numbers (Dt 7:7), or strength (Dt 8:17), or uprightness (Dt 9:4), but solely justified on the basis that God 'loved you and meant to keep the oath which he swore to your ancestors' (Dt 7:8). Therefore at the beginning of Israel there is the tender 'yes' of a God who, prior to any response, bestows grace. Being chosen because of love alone is grace. 'When Israel was a child I loved him, and I called my son out of Egypt... I myself taught Ephraim to walk, I myself took them by the arm... [I] was leading them with human ties, with leading-strings of love...

with them, I was like someone lifting an infant to his cheek... I bent down to feed him' (Ho 11:1, 3-4).

Being led into a land where 'milk and honey flow' is grace. 'I brought you to a country of plenty, to enjoy its produce and good things' (Jr 2:7). Again, the gift of a law which constitutes 'a kingdom of priests, a holy nation' (Ex 19:6) is grace. A nation to whom the 'distant' and the 'spotless' one — such is the meaning of holy — has made himself close, so that by following his decrees Israel might itself become an uncontaminated people, a living remembrance among the nations of what happens when God walks alongside: life bears fruit in justice and mercy (Mi 6:8).

Israel and Mary, Mary and Israel refer each to the other.

The one, Israel, is the chosen nation on which, through sheer good-will and in view of the Covenant, the grace of beauty has been bestowed, rendering it attractive in the sight of God. 'I saw you as I was passing... I bathed you in water... I loaded you with jewels... You grew more and more beautiful; and you rose to be queen. The fame of your beauty spread through the nations, since it was perfect, because I had clothed you with my own splendour... (Ezk 16:8-14). 'I shall betroth you to myself for ever, I shall betroth you in uprightness and justice, and faithful love and tenderness. Yes, I shall betroth you to myself in loyalty and in the knowledge of Yahweh' (Ho 2:21-22).

The other, Mary, enfolded in a tenderness which rendered her attractive and beautiful, in view of the birth on earth of the Son, bearing a new and more perfect Covenant, is Israel led back in the Spirit to an original beauty, one not dimmed by infidelity, as is witnessed by the *fiat* so positively awaited at the Annunciation.

Contemplation of the 'graced one', while introducing us into the mystery of Israel, whose figure and fulfilment she is, also inaugurates a deep understanding of the Church and of Christians, whose most pure archetype and first-fruit she is.

The graced ones

Once again, the love which determined the choice of Mary, replica of Israel, is the same love which determines the choice of the Church. Titus 2:11-14 and 3:3-9 can be taken as the key to a good ecclesial explanation of Luke 1:28.

The source from which every gift springs is the *grace (charis)* of God, that is to say his goodness, his love for humanity, his mercy and his loving tenderness shown in 'our great God and Saviour Christ Jesus' (Tt 2:13), in him who is 'full of grace and truth' (Jn 1:14).

The God who draws closer to Mary through the angel is the same one who makes himself neighbour to each person through Jesus Christ, gracing them in order to render them attractive and, through the Spirit who is God's power for rebirth and renewal (Tt 3:5-6), making them blossom into new creatures. Such new creatures are open to eternal life and live now in justice, with zeal for good works (Tt 2:14; 3:1,8,14). They are 'glorious, with no speck or wrinkle or anything like that, but holy and faultless' (Ep 5:27); chosen 'to be holy and faultless before him in love' (Ep 1:4), each one bearing their own gift *(charisma)* for the common good.

Contemplation of the *kecharitomene* (graced one) therefore leads to the heart of the biblical message which is synthesised and contained in Luke 1:28. Such an announcement is the loving face of a God who passes bestowing grace, moved by a limitless mercy which restores beauty.

Through the words of the angel to Mary, 'Rejoice, you who were rendered pleasing' in the eyes of your Lord by the Lord himself, those undertaking *lectio divina* see in her the recapitulation accomplished within Israel of the Church and of themselves. She represents all whom the Father has graced in passing, by whispering to our hearts in the risen Jesus 'you have been made attractive' and 'beautiful' simply on account of a gift of love, without any merit.

This is an absolutely gratuitous favour, for Mary in view of her giving birth to the Light, and for the Church and us in view of our giving witness to the same Light, either by the holiness of an undefiled life of charity or by the joyful *Magnificat* which breaks forth uncontainably from the hearts of those upon whom grace has been bestowed.

But, regarding all we have said: 'how can this come about?' (Lk 1:34). Mary's question becomes our own and the reply of the angel to Mary becomes the reply directed to each one of us: 'The Lord is with you.'

THE LORD IS WITH YOU

History of vocations

The expression *The Lord is with you* forms part of the repertory of history of vocations. It was already used in relation to Isaac (Gn 26:24) and Jacob (Gn 28:15) and the formula corresponds to the divine reply to those who have been called but who put up difficulties in accepting the mission entrusted to them.

'Yahweh then said, "...So now I am sending you to Pharaoh, for you to bring my people the Israelites out of Egypt." Moses said to God, "Who am I to go to Pharaoh and bring the Israelites out of Egypt?" "*I shall be with you...*"' (Ex 3:7,10-12).

'Moses said to Yahweh, "Please, my Lord, I have never been eloquent"... Yahweh said to him..."Now go, I shall help you speak and instruct you what to say"' (Ex 4:10-12).

'The Angel of Yahweh came and sat under the terebinth at Ophrah which belonged to Joash of Abiezer. Gideon his son was threshing wheat inside the winepress, to keep it hidden from Midian, and the Angel of Yahweh appeared to him and said, "*Yahweh is with you*... Go in this strength of yours, and you will rescue Israel from the power of Midian. Am I not sending you myself?" Gideon replied, "Forgive me, my lord, but how can I deliver Israel? My clan is the weakest in Manasseh and I am the least important of my father's family." Yahweh replied, "*I shall be with you* and you will crush Midian as though it were one man" ' (Jg 6:11-12,14-16).

'The word of Yahweh came to me, saying: "Before I formed you in the womb I knew you; before you came to birth I consecrated you; I appointed you as prophet to the nations." I then said, "Ah, ah, ah, Lord Yahweh; you see, I do not know how to speak: I am only a child!" But Yahweh replied, "Do not say: I am only a child, for you must go to all to whom I send you and say whatever I command you. Do not be afraid of confronting them, for *I am with you* to rescue you" ' (Jr 1:4-8).

Placed in the context of accounts of vocation, and Luke 1:26-38 is one such, the words '*The Lord is with you*' are linked with Mary's objection: 'But how can this come about, since I have no knowledge of man?' (Lk 1:34) and integrated into the angel's reply: 'The Holy Spirit will come upon you, and the power of the Most High will cover you with its shadow' (Lk 1:35). Approached by Gabriel, who announces to her the decision of God to make her the mother of the Son of the Most High, of the Son of God (Lk 1:32,35), a vocation which surpasses all imagining, Mary is disturbed (Lk 1:28) and protests her own littleness (Lk 1:48) and her own choice of life, virginity (Lk 1:34).

To these objections, God responds by showing himself as the Omnipotent One, able to accomplish great things in her (Lk 1:49) by means of the creative power of the Spirit. This means having God with her, God for whom 'nothing is impossible' (Lk 1:37).

God who allots the task is able to bring it to completion, wherever his strong presence is not hindered. In fact, it is from the joining of *The Lord is with you* – 'Let it happen to me as you have said' (Lk 1:28,38) that 'salvation... a light of revelation for the Gentiles and glory for your people Israel' (Lk 2:30,32) takes flesh.

Moreover, reading the expression *The Lord is with you* in the context of vocation-events immediately broadens the horizons of our contemplation of Mary, the one who recapitulates the vocation of Israel from its origins, who sums up individual vocations and who focuses the poor of Yahweh.

The chosen race, nameless and inconsequential in the list of nations (Dt 7:7), finds its supreme expression in the humble Virgin and in her absolute marginality. The extraordinary calls of Moses, Gideon and Jeremiah in view of particular tasks attain an unforeseen, unheard of and indescribable fullness in the vocation of Mary to divine motherhood.

We rediscover the astonishment, the deep sense of incapacity faced with the commission received, the courage to object and the free and unconditional surrender of the three chosen ones in the maiden of Nazareth, brought to fulfilment. Though deeply disturbed, she nevertheless professes her own *humilitas* (humility) and *virginitas* (virginity) as real difficulties in the way of the actualization of God's message in her. Not afraid but with courage she braces herself up to question and with trust she declares herself totally at the service of her Lord. These are indications of a way of standing in the presence of God which is quite different both from an irrational negation of oneself as a drop which mingles in the ocean and loses its own identity and, from a proud denial of him in order to affirm one's own judgements.

First of all, Mary listens, then she questions and finally she accepts and sings, offers herself freely and joyfully as the servant of the Lord (Lk 1:38), the cream of the poor of Yahweh, of those who have unreservedly surrendered themselves to the one whom they have not denied. And he for his part, attracted by their humility, not only does not ravish their virginity, but makes it fruitful. This happens where *The Lord is with you.*

Vocation and the Spirit

In the calling of the Virgin, the Church contemplates its own vocation. Her marginality outstrips that of those chosen by the Father in Jesus Christ, both in Israel and among the nations.

Addressing the twelve tribes dispersed throughout the world, James writes: 'Listen, my dear brothers: it was those who were poor according to the world that God chose, to be rich in faith and to be the heirs to the kingdom which he promised to those who love him' (Jm 2:5).

In his turn, Paul admonishes the proud in the Church at Corinth as follows. 'Consider, brothers, how you were called; not many of you are wise by human standards, not many influential, not many from noble families. No, God chose those who by human standards are fools to shame the wise; he chose those who by human reckoning are weak to shame the strong, those who in human esteem are common and contemptible – indeed those who count for nothing – to reduce to nothing all those that do count for something, so that no human being might feel boastful before God' (1 Co 1:26-29).

By contemplating the humble servant of the Lord, the people of Israel and the Church *(Ecclesia)* are brought back to the roots of their calling: the loving act of a Father who stoops and calls 'littleness' to himself.

This convocation is similar to Mary's: to accomplish a 'great thing'. One was called to become the mother of a Son, generated, given, announced and followed until Easter; the other is sent to give a living, proclaimed and sung witness to the love which has appeared in that same Son, who 'although he was rich,... became poor for your sake, so that you should become rich through his poverty' (2 Co 8:9).

The clear awareness of one's own 'worldly' insignificance serves the extraordinary and universal good news: 'this is how God loved the world: he gave his only Son' (Jn 3:16), an utterly unique gift through Mary and a gift given by *martyria* (witness) through the Church, so that all people might find joy.

Awareness of its own freely accepted insignificance in terms of worldly prestige is an indispensable condition if the Church is to rediscover its own original mandate in the midst of humanity. 'I have neither silver nor gold, but I will give you what I have: in the name of Jesus Christ the Nazarene, walk! Then he took him by the right hand...' (Ac 3:6-7). Only a Church which is faithful to its own statute of poverty and passionately faithful to the mandate it has received is able truly to take by the hand the casualties of life, and to do it without presumption.

The Virgin's 'how can this come about' was re-lived by the primitive community in Jerusalem, in which she was present (Ac 1:14). This community began with the recognition that there is no witness except in the Spirit: 'but you will receive the power of the Holy Spirit which will come on you, and then you will be my witnesses not only in Jerusalem but throughout Judaea and Samaria, and indeed to earth's remotest end' (Ac 1:8). The descent of the Spirit upon Mary and upon the Church is nothing other than the actualization of the expression: *The Lord is with you*, in order that the wish of God might become a reality. In the Spirit, Mary will give birth to the Son; in the Spirit, the Church will proclaim him in every corner of the earth. A journey in song: the *Magnificat* accompanies the steps of those who bear the glad tidings.

Therefore the words *The Lord is with you*

contain and reveal a meaning which goes beyond the daily *Dominus vobiscum* (The Lord be with you). They take us back to the sources of the vocation of Israel, Moses, Gideon, Jeremiah, Mary and the Church; a calling which is realizable only where the power of the Spirit is not turned into sadness (cf. Is 63:10; Ep 4:30). These vocations reflect the great vocation, that of the Christ, born of the Spirit, baptized in the Spirit, sent by the Spirit and giver of the Spirit.

To become aware of all this in surrender to the one who calls is to enter the realm of blessing and to stand already now in clear and final attendance upon the 'Lord with us'. 'Look, here God lives among human beings. He will make his home among them; they will be his people, and he will be their God, God-with-them. He will wipe away all tears from their eyes; there will be no more death, and no more mourning or sadness or pain. The world of the past has gone' (Rv 21:3-4).

BLESSED AMONG WOMEN

Blessing-Benediction

The term *blessing* (*eulogia* in Greek, *berakah* in Hebrew), conceals and reveals a double movement: descending and ascending. In the first case what is underlined is the loving descent of a God who draws close 'speaking well' [cf. benediction], that is to say, uttering words and performing actions of kindness towards those who enjoy his favour. In the second case what is noted is the human response which rises to a God who is well spoken of, praising him and thanking him for his gifts.

It follows that there is no term comparable with benediction for clarifying the relation of God to humanity and vice versa. Innumerable examples run throughout Scripture; a good example is Ephesians 1:3 which roundly summarizes what has been said. 'Blessed be the God and Father of our Lord Jesus Christ, who has blessed us with all the spiritual blessings of heaven in Christ.'

'Blessed be God', which corresponds to

'giving thanks with joy to the Father' in Colossians 1:12, is the praising (doxological) and thanking (eucharistic) response to the free initiative of God who has always, and radically in Christ, come to us showering us with every blessing: life, food, political ransom, purpose, husbands and wives, children and friends, health and strength in tribulation, forgiveness of sins, being chosen, being called to holiness, the Holy Spirit and eternal life.

The conclusion is self-evident. In the 'faith experience' of the biblical world, God stands amidst humanity bestowing blessing, prompted solely by his generous will (Ep 1:5 – *eudokía*) and by grace (Ep 1:6-7 – *charis*) poured out in abundance through his beloved Son (Ep 1:8); and humanity stands before God likewise giving blessing, prompted solely by wonder translated into hymns of praise and prayers of thanksgiving (Col 3:15; 2 Co 4:15; Ep 5:20). It is not by chance that Mary perfectly exemplifies the mutual relation expressed in the word 'benediction', for she is the figure of Israel and the image of the Church, the glorifier of the Most High who has done great things in her (Lk 1:46,49). She who is the blessed.

She who is blessed

'Most blessed of women be Jael... may she be most blessed!' we read in Judges 5:24; and in Judith 13:18 it says: 'May you be blessed, my daughter, by God Most High, beyond all women on earth'. The song of Deborah and the proclamation of Uzziah continue in the hymn of Elizabeth in whose exclamation (Lk 1:42 – *anaphonein,* a word used in the Septuagint for liturgical music) with 'a loud cry' is contained the praise of Mary rendered by the believers of Israel and by the early Church: 'Of all women you are the most blessed (*eulogemene*)' (Lk 1:42). This praise has been perpetuated down the centuries: 'from now onwards all generations will call me blessed' (Lk 1:48).

At first sight, this assertion seems to contradict what has been said about benediction by introducing into it a new element, the exaltation of a creature to the detriment of the one and only glorification of the Father through Jesus Christ in the Spirit and in the communion of saints. In fact it is not so.

The congratulation, the 'speaking well' and celebration of Mary contained in the 'blessed' of Elizabeth and of all generations, both in the intimacy of each heart and spoken out in public liturgy, are really a doxological canticle to God celebrated not only in himself and for himself but also in his own works, in which he rejoices (Ps 103[104]:31).

In this case the work of God is Mary, the woman in whom the tender strength of the Father's blessing has accomplished the 'great thing' of conceiving in the Spirit and bringing to birth in the world the 'Saviour' who is 'Christ the Lord' (Lk 2:11), 'a light of revelation for the gentiles and the glory of your people Israel' (Lk 2:32), the Son in whom 'all humanity will see the salvation of God' (Lk 3:6).

Mary is the woman who embodies femininity open to God and his plan: Jael, Judith, Sarah, Rebecca, Leah, Rachel, Tamar, Rahab, Bathsheba, Ruth, Anna and Elizabeth. A femininity which is at once 'just and sinning', redeemed, by sheer grace, in the *Pneumatophoric* Virgin named Mary, bearer of the Spirit.

Therefore, in her who is blessed there occurs the fusion of God's gracious action and absolute human praise of God himself:

– 'blessed' because favoured by a Father who has made her lovable and who is with her in the Spirit for the achievement of her divine motherhood;

– 'blessed' because made worthy of praise by a Father who is not jealous but happy to see his completed work honoured and *hymned*, aware that all praise of her cannot but turn into benediction of himself, who is her author.

Praise of the Virgin, like celebration of the saints, is fundamentally an event in the Spirit. God himself gives the former and offers the latter to his Church and to humanity as a whole, to signal what happens wherever his Presence is not unwelcome: the 'new creation' emerges. In praising it the Father is honoured, just as in contemplating and extolling a forest decked in autumn gold the sun is celebrated as its author. One glorifies God also by honouring his friends.

In this perspective, benediction as a doxological event always ends up by returning to the source from which all benediction descends, as the Saragossa Ecumenical Declaration of 1979 well understood: 'We acknowledge in common that all Christian praise is praise of God in Christ. If we praise the saints, and in particular the Virgin Mary as the Mother of God, this praise is rendered essentially to the glory of God who, in glorifying the saints crowns his own gifts' (cf. Preface of Holy Men and Women I). Praise of the saints includes and always returns us to the 'thrice Holy' who brought them into being; celebrating them is giving glory to God.

Finally, Mary is blessed 'among all women', a Semitic turn of phrase which seeks to point to her being blessed *par excellence*, the most blessed because only she was chosen to become in a unique way the Mother of God in the Spirit.

It seems that we can say that 'blessed' stands right at the heart of the *Hail Mary* and is its full exegesis. Blessed because visited by a God who has showered her with gifts: joy, grace, motherhood and the praise of all generations to the honour and glory of God himself.

This blessing is not taken lightly but received in faith; because of this it is a source of joy within Mary the believer, as again the hymn of Elizabeth underlines. 'Yes, blessed is she who believed that the promise made her by the Lord would be fulfilled' (Lk 1:45).

We who are blessed

In her who is blessed, the purest image of the Church, every creature is called to know and feel that they are blessed, loved like her by a Father who, pouring forth the Spirit, the great blessing, opens the way to a life in the light (Mt 5:16), in the footsteps of the Son, the Blessed One. In her who is blessed, everyone of us is called to:

A luminous existence, blessed because under the sign of a love which opens the creature to the Abba, to friendship, to life and to songs of praise and thanksgiving, having destroyed every 'harmful image' of God, of man, of daily life and of death.

An existence in the light, blessed because free from boastfulness (1 Co 1:29) and from receiving empty praise (Jn 5:44), content with all praise which becomes glorification of the Father who is in heaven (Mt 5:16).

A luminous existence, blessed because it is open even amid sorrow and weariness to the unspeakable joy which comes from the knowledge of being loved by a Father, who is constantly thanked, and of being blessed by the Blessed One.

Finally, to everyone is offered the possibility to become like Mary, the blessed one who glorifies, the woman from whom is born a fruit of blessing.

BLESSED IS THE FRUIT OF YOUR WOMB, JESUS

She is blessed in view of the Blessed One

The promise of blessing made to the faithful Israel, 'You will be blessed in the town and blessed in the countryside; blessed, the offspring of your body' (Dt 28:4), finds its fulfilment in 'blessed is the fruit of your womb' (Lk 1:42), said by Elizabeth to the faithful Virgin daughter of Zion.

The aging relative, Elizabeth, having become the voice which initiates and sums up in song the spiritual understanding of the events (Lk 1:48), immediately adds 'and blessed is the fruit' to the 'you are the most blessed'. This is an addition of the utmost importance because it strongly underlines the inseparability of the mother and son, womb and fruit of the womb, both placed under the sign of blessing, which is to say of God's favour and of believers' praise.

More precisely, the coming of Mary, the blessed one, the chosen, the beloved, the bearer of the Spirit, overflowing with beauty, is in view of the coming of the Blessed One par excellence and as such its prelude and prefiguration. He is the chosen (Lk 9:35), the beloved (Lk 3:22), the *pneumatophor* (full of the Spirit) (Lk 3:22) who is constituted as the source of universal blessing with the outpouring of the Spirit (Ac 2:33) upon Israel (Ac 3:25-26) and on all flesh, thus accomplishing the promise made to Abraham (Ga 3:8-14).

In the same way, the doxological proclamation of Mary's blessedness and happiness does not exhaust itself in her but, before it finally reaches the Father (Ep 1:3), extends to the fruit of her womb, named Jesus. He is blessed by Elizabeth at the time of his conception-birth; by the crowd in the days of his entry into Jerusalem: 'Blessed is he who is coming in the name of the Lord!' (Mk 11:9) and by heaven and earth from the moment of his entry into God's world without end: 'Worthy is the Lamb that was sacrificed to receive power, riches, wisdom, strength, honour, glory and blessing... To the One seated on the throne and to the Lamb, be all praise, honour, glory and power, for ever and ever' (Rv 5:12-13).

In the pairing 'she-who-is-blessed'-blessed/fruit (*benedicta-benedictus*) we are introduced to the idea of never separating what God has united: she is loved in view of the beloved Son, she is graced in view of the source of grace and she is praised in view of the great doxology to the Son and in him to the Father in the Spirit.

Jesus

Why do we proclaim Jesus blessed? The reason is contained in his very name which means 'Yahweh saves', 'God saves'. We cannot but praise him who has been given to us as Saviour (Lk 2:11) in a unique way: 'of all the names in the world given to men, this is the only one by which we can be saved' (Ac 4:12).

From him, 'the rising Sun' who 'has come from on high to visit us, to give light to *those who live in darkness and the shadow dark as death*' (Lk 1:79), we receive the Spirit who, by bringing the Word alive in us, opens the way to the knowledge of God, to an eternal inheritance, to forgiveness (Ac 26:16-18), to communion of hearts and goods (Ac 2:42; 4:32) and to the ability to bless and 'speak well', overthrowing all barriers of discrimination. 'But I say this to you who are listening: Love your enemies, do good to those who hate you, bless those who curse you, pray for those who treat you badly' (Lk 6:27-28). In this way, 'you will be children of the Most

High, for he himself is kind to the ungrateful and the wicked.' 'Be compassionate just as your Father is compassionate' (Lk 6:35-36).

What was said now come to pass: through her, the blessed, the Father offers humanity the 'blessed-Saviour', who in turn pours out the Spirit he has received, the power of God who enables life to blossom in blessedness and the present to be redeemed from meaninglessness and opened up to doing good for friends and enemies, beyond all logic and divisive behaviour.

This is the way that leads to the incomparable gift of the Kingdom. 'Never repay one wrong with another, or one abusive word with another; instead, repay with a blessing. That is what you are called to do, so that you inherit a blessing' (1 Pt 3:9).

At the heart of the Hail Mary

Therefore, it is not by chance that at the end of the first part of the *Hail Mary*, at its heart, the Church in liturgical use has added the name of Jesus. He is its clear explanation.

She who is called to rejoice, the graced one in whom beauty abides, she who has God with her, in short she who is blessed, is such in view of the fount of joy, the source of grace, the blessed Son in whom God visits us and saves us by placing our days within the heaven of benediction.

Feeling ourselves to be blessed means knowing ourselves to have been touched by the Spirit of love, a Spirit perceived as forgiveness, as power opening us to universal gentleness and as a voice whispering to our depths their eternal being. Having been constituted the abode of the Spirit of the Lord Jesus like blessed Mary, we who are blessed cannot but announce and proclaim this good news and this name, both to the waiting Israel (Lk 1:39-46) and to every land and nation (Mt 2:1-12).

HOLY MARY

*From her who is holy to the
'thrice Holy'*

The second part of the *Hail Mary* is a petition which begins by qualifying Mary to whom the prayer is addressed as *holy*. This qualification has its explanation in what has been already said: the loved one who has been graced has the Holy Father with her (Lk 1:28), the Holy Spirit in her (Lk 1:35) and the Son, the Holy One (Lk 1:35; Ac 3:14), taking flesh from her flesh.

The dwelling of the Holy One is herself constituted holy by the generous graciousness of God.

Thus it is that reflecting on the invocation 'Holy Mary' we are immediately led to contemplate the 'thrice Holy' who has caused her to participate in his sanctity.

Far off

There is no term which can compare with 'holy' for defining the identity and the sublime truth of the Judaeo-Christian God. Thus the heavenly court hymns him: 'holy, holy, holy is the Lord God, the Almighty' (Rv 4:8; Is 6:3). Thus the voice of the Law proclaims him: 'I, Yahweh your God, am holy' (Lv 19:2). Thus the Church on earth in the eucharistic celebration confesses him: 'holy holy, holy'.

The thrice holy, Father-Son-Spirit, alone is the *holy*, that is to say, as the Hebraic root of the word underlines, the one 'apart', 'distinct' from the world and from humanity, 'inviolable'.

A distinction of *essence* and *existence*. He who says of himself 'I am God, not man' (Ho 11:9), is he 'who alone is immortal, whose home is in inaccessible light, whom no human being has seen or is able to see' (1 Tm 6:16). He is the being of whom it is written: 'my thoughts are not your thoughts and your ways are not my ways'. 'For the heavens are as high above earth as my ways are above your ways, my thoughts above your thoughts' (Is 55:8-9). In fact, 'God is no human being that he should lie, no child of Adam to change his mind. Is it his to say and not to do, is it his to speak and not fulfil?' (Nb 23:19).

Proclaiming the holiness of God therefore means recognising, first of all, his radical and constitutive otherness with regard to the universe and humanity. Neither a cog within the first, nor a work of the hands, mind or heart of the second, God is beyond all human imag-ining and every human desire in his immortal and invisible brilliance; and beyond all human conduct in his definitive and constant innocence and goodness (Lk 18:19).

He indeed is the Holy One, the Presence haloed in light who dwells in silence, inaccessible, indescribable and with no shadow of evil.

Before this ineffable Beauty, invisible and indescribable, all that remains is adoring wonder and sacred respect. This should be translated into rigorous discipline in order not to violate the mystery and the secrecy with illusory and deceptive images and discourses, which simply project our needs and our desires—Idols.

However, the urgency of recovering this dimension of the otherness of God and of speaking about him with extreme sobriety is something which is asserting itself in an age in which, on one side, the ways of psycho-analysis, socio-politics and science and, on the other, the return to biblical, liturgical and Patristic sources, have strongly contributed to unmasking and encouraging the downfall of the gods substituted for the 'thrice Holy'.

Near to sanctify

Though the aspect of otherness is fundamental, it does not exhaust the unfathomable richness of the mystery of God.

The never ending parable of the believing Israel has proclaimed and continues at various times to proclaim that the far off, the distant, the Other, the sinless, in short the Holy One, loves to come forth from his inaccessibility in order to make himself close, near and present. In fact, it is written: 'I am... the Holy One in your midst' (Ho 11:9), who has come to you in order to make you 'a holy nation' (Ex 19:6); therefore, 'Be holy, for I, Yahweh your God, am holy' (Lv 19:2).

Which means: among the nations tied to a multiplicity of idols constructed by humanity, be witnesses to my Name which has always drawn existence and immortality from itself. Among the nations subject to a multiplicity of directions, be the witnesses to my Way, the only one which bestows direction and authenticity on the days of humanity.

Holy, then, is the people which has with it the Distant One and his Way; it is initiated into standing as a holy nation among the nations, both near and distant: near because mingling with them, distant because alien to their idols and their idolatrous ways, herald of the newness that occurs wherever the Other is welcomed: life becomes quite different from what it was.

This then is the particular though often unexpected vocation of the believing Israel, on to which the Christian witness is grafted, itself often marred by infidelity. Nevertheless, it is a witness called to confess and proclaim that the Invisible has become fully visible in the face of the Son (Jn 14:9). The Indescribable has become perfect speech in the Word made flesh (Jn 1:14), revealing to all the project hidden in God from the foundation of the world: to take a dwelling deep within humanity and there to set down the 'code of holiness', the word-commandment of love (Jn 14:23-24).

In the Son and in the power of the Spirit the Holy Father, spanning the infinite distance which separates every human being from himself, by sheer grace offers every creature his Presence of light and his commandment of light. So that, in the footsteps of his Son, every being might become a child of the light and the whole of humanity become 'a holy nation' (1 Pt 2:9), reflecting the holy face of the Father which has appeared in Jesus Christ, the face of the one crucified and transfigured, mirror of the impeccable action of the Father through carrying out his word in the Spirit (1 Jn 2:20, 25; 3:9).

Holy Mary

While it contemplates and invokes the Virgin as 'holy', the Christian community, in being led back to the source from which all holiness comes forth, is also introduced to an understanding of the sublime Christian vocation.

In Mary, the perfect Israel and purest image of the Church, the call to holiness achieved its complete fulfilment. In her, the Holy One found full acceptance, bestowing light and beauty upon her. In her who is 'sublime because uplifted' – which is the meaning of the name Mary – the hallowed word of the Holy One found an unconditional Yes, giving rise to a life which, even though humble and crossed by grief, was transparent.

In 'Holy Mary', sister and mother, the Church of sinners sees what it must be and the sign of how to approach it: by not letting pass the visit of him who comes from afar to make our life 'holy and faultless before him in love' (Ep 1:4). In order to achieve this, let us not be afraid to entrust ourselves to her intercession: 'pray for us sinners' called as we are to bring about in history, by holiness of life, the presence of the 'thrice Holy'.

MOTHER OF GOD

Theotòkos

The expression 'mother of God' contains Mary's *raison d'être*. The Father has graced her, favoured her and made her holy so that she might become *Theotòkos, Dei Genetrix*, Mother of God, the creature who brings God into the world.

Even though the form of these terms, which was officially sealed at Ephesus in 431 AD, is not scriptural, their substance is. A single line of reflection, starting from Paul and reaching John via Luke, brings us back to them. Thus the basic affirmation of Paul: 'when the completion of the time came, God sent his Son, born of a woman...' (Ga 4:4), to which the Church has returned in prayer, is better understood.

The woman's name is Mary (Lk 1:27) and the event of the Spirit, who is the creative power of God abiding in her and making the perfectly obedient one's (Lk 1:38) virgin body fruitful (Lk 1:27), is the conception and birth of Jesus the Messiah (Lk 1:31-32), the Son of

God (Lk 1:35) and the Lord (Lk 1:43). In Mary his mother (Jn 2:1), the Word who is eternal and divine in nature (Jn 1:1) took flesh and lived among us (Jn 1:14). Therefore, in the words of an Orthodox theologian, 'By the inconceivable mystery of the Incarnation of the *Logos* [Word]', Mary is 'rightly and truly' called *Theotòkos* [mother of God].

Mary gave birth not simply to a divine man *(theophoros)* nor to a divinised man, but to the 'only begotten Son of God', who became son of man so that man might become son of God (Ga 4:5). The great mystery is hymned as follows by the Orthodox liturgy of the Synaxis of the Mother of God. 'He who before the morning star was begotten of the Father without a mother, has this day taken flesh on earth in you [Mary] without a father; therefore a star announces him to the magi, while the angels sing with the shepherds the immaculate birth you have given, O full of grace' (Matins).

Before such an event of grace and salvation, which makes of Mary the one 'who gave to the world the Life that renews all things' (*Lumen Gentium,* 56) and the dawn which brought forth the sun of justice, we can only give thanks with wonder and ask further for light to understand it more deeply.

Wonderful exchange

Manifold reflections arise from con-templation of her who is called and in-voked as the 'mother of God', and from the glance portrayed in any of the icons of the *Theotòkos* which are so numerous.

The *first* refers to the creation scene when 'Yahweh God shaped man from the soil of the ground and blew the breath of life into his nostrils, and man became a living being' (Gen 2:7). A scene which occurred at the beginning in view of the birth in the fullness of time of the new and perfect Adam, from the believing and undefiled body of one called Mary, by the vivifying Spirit of the Father.

The *Theotòkos* suggests the fulfilment of the project of creation; the soil of the ground, the breath and the appearance of Adam are the first stage in a process which looks and waits to find its fulfilment in the virgin ground called Mary, recapitulation of the cosmos and of humanity, the Holy Spirit who proceeds from the Father, and Christ Jesus of whom it was said 'Here is the man' (Jn 19:5). In him, in view of whom everything was made (Col 1:16), creation is accomplished.

The *second* considers the wonderful exchange of natures which took place in Mary. It was in her womb that the Father gave earthly existence to the eternal Word whose nature is divine; it was in her womb that the Father gave immortality and divinisation to human nature, uniting it with the divine nature of the Word with the strictest regard for their difference.

In the Lord Jesus, true God and true man, divinity and humanity are joined in eternal wedlock; the nativity, the moment of God's entry and assumption of humanity through the Virgin, refers to the ascension, the moment of the definitive entry of transfigured humanity into God by way of the cross. The *Theotókos* is the undefiled space which freely gave place to the wedding in the Word of the two natures and the humanity which joyfully gave flesh to the divine Word. From that moment the Word who has always had a Father, also had a mother.

Retaining a lively memory of the 'mother of God', means never losing the recollection of what happened in her, the humanization of God and the divinisation of humanity in Jesus Christ, something absolutely unique and never heard of before. The Orthodox liturgy has well understood it. 'A wondrous event is taking place: God is becoming man. He has remained what he was and has assumed what he was not without undergoing either confusion or division.' And man becomes god.

Once again: 'How can this great mystery be told? The bodiless takes a body; the Word takes the burden of flesh upon himself; the invisible makes himself seen, the immaterial lets himself be touched; he who is without beginning begins; the Son of God becomes son of man: Jesus Christ, the same yesterday, today and for ever'.

The *third* reflection is even more disconcerting. The All-Powerful and 'Wholly Other', in the Son who is born of Mary, shows himself to humanity as a dependent baby, defenceless, in want and needing care and affection. The fount of love begs for love, the rich master of the worlds asks for bread, he who adorns the lilies and the flowers of the field needs clothes and liberty itself makes submission.

'He went down with them then and came to Nazareth and lived under their authority' (Lk 2:51), becoming obedient even unto death. We read in a hymn of the apostolic Church: '[Jesus Christ] being in the form of God... emptied himself, taking the form of a slave, becoming as human beings are; and being in every way like a human being, he was humbler yet, even to accepting death, death on a cross' (Ph 2:6-8).

In the 'mother of God' there is formed a Son who shows himself to humanity alike in all things except sin and who begins by accepting its infancy. In the secret hope of not instilling fear, of being welcomed simply as a friend, as a companion on the way, who knocks at the door of the human heart to communicate as like unto like the great gift of the Father, the Spirit who opens the way to sonship and inheritance.

'[But] when the completion of the time came, God sent his Son, born of a woman,... so that we could receive adoption as sons. As you are sons, God has sent into our hearts the Spirit of his Son crying "Abba, Father"; and so you are no longer a slave, but a son; and if a son, then an heir, by God's own act' (Ga 4:4-7).

Mother and image of the Church

Finally, contemplation of the mother of God becomes understanding of the secret of the Church, of the Christian and in principle of everyone. She who is full of the Spirit refers to the Church born at Pentecost and to the Christian, temple of the Spirit. She who has within her the Son and who brings him forth, giving him to Israel, the poor and just, represented by the shepherds and by Elizabeth, symbolises the Church at the moment of offering to every creature the great gift of the

Father abiding within it, bringing him forth, as it were, by the threefold witness of word, life and blood.

The mother who gives birth to God as a baby and cares for him and who at Cana suggests 'Do whatever he tells you', reflects the Church called to bring forth sons like the Son for the Father, by baptism in water and the Spirit, so as then to feed them on the Word made flesh in the Eucharist. The Church which at the same time is attentive to the concrete needs of all the poor and the little ones under the sun.

The examples could continue. To look with a clear, loving and strong gaze at the *Theotōkos* is without doubt quietly to perceive something of the mystery of God and of humanity. It is to perceive also something of the 'feminine dimension' of the Church, called to accept the seed of the Spirit, to bring forth and feed the Son and never to lose the recollection of how indispensable he is and how essential it is radically to follow him. As the Preface of the Assumption says, Mary herself is 'the beginning and the pattern'.

To us Jesus gave her as mother, to her we sinners turn asking for her intercession: 'Pray for us sinners'.

PRAY FOR US SINNERS

The great intercessor

Sinners address themselves to 'Holy Mary', that she might pray for them. A legitimate request which needs to be set in the broad context of prayer of intercession in order to be understood properly, starting from the unequivocal recognition of the Lord Jesus as the one great intercessor, who cannot be substituted.

Jesus while on earth prayed for Simon: 'Simon, Simon! Look, Satan has got his wish to sift you all like wheat; but I have prayed for you, Simon, that your faith may not fail, and once you have recovered, you in your turn must strengthen your brothers' (Lk 2:31-32).

He prays that the Paraclete may be sent to the disciples and for their safekeeping and unity. 'I shall ask the Father, and he will give you another Paraclete to be with you for ever, the Spirit of truth...' (Jn 14:16-17). 'It is for them that I pray... [Keep] those you have given me true to your name, so that they may be one like us... [I am asking you] to protect them from the Evil One' (Jn 17: 9,11,15).

He prays for all those who will believe. 'I pray not only for these but also for those who through their teaching will come to believe in me. May they all be one' (Jn 17:20-21).

He prays for his own killers. 'Father, forgive them; they do not know what they are doing' (Lk 23:34).

The *risen Lord*, seated at the right hand of God continues this intercessory work of his.

The witness of the Letter to the Romans, the Letter to the Hebrews and the first Letter of John is explicit. 'Christ Jesus, who died – yes and more, who was raised from the dead and is at God's right hand – is adding his plea for us' (Rm 8:34). 'It follows, then, that his power to save those who come to God through him is absolute, since he lives for ever to intercede for them' (Heb 7:25). 'My children, I am writing this to prevent you from sinning; but if anyone does sin, we have an advocate with the Father, Jesus Christ, the upright' (1 Jn 2:1).

For its part, the Church of all times and places has known that its own prayer of petition reaches the Father only through the one intercessor, Jesus. The 'Through our Lord Jesus Christ' with which liturgical prayers end has assimilated well the teaching of the Master referred to in John's gospel: 'so that the

Father will give you anything you ask him in my name' (Jn 15:16).

The Church, the Body of Christ who intercedes

The Lord is not isolated. Ascended into the communion of the Trinity with his transfigured humanity, he possesses as well an earthly body which is called the Church. 'Now Christ's body is yourselves, each of you with a part to play in the whole.' (1 Co 12:27) Living members made to participate in the adoration of the Father in the Spirit of truth (Jn 4:23-24), that is to say, we are, through the Son and associated with him, made capable of a relationship with God, like that of the Son who is the truth.

Therefore, moved by his Spirit, Christians are focused, with him and like him, on the Father, accepting the Father's love and word and responding to him with attention, praise and intercession. From this intercession no one and nothing is excluded: all human beings and their rulers (1 Tm 2:1-2), the Churches (2 Co 13:7, 9; 9:14; Ep 1:16; Ph 1:4,9; Col 1:3; 4:12), preachers (Col 4:3), persecutors (Mt 5:44; Lk 6:28), individuals (Rm 15:30; 2 Tm 1:3), the sick (Jn 5:14), sinners and the whole world with its animals and plants.

The love abiding in the heart of the Lord Jesus and poured out in abundance over his friends opens the way to a solidarity such as to become an appeal for universal salvation through Christ, with Christ and in Christ. Praying one for another and interceding for all forms part of the essential constitution of the Church. It explains and expresses the communion of saints and their fellowship as guardians, as the voice of the apostolic Church recalls on various occasions: 'the heartfelt prayer of someone upright works very powerfully' (Jm 5:16).

That is why the same voice urges prayer for one another (Ep 6:18; 2 Co 9:14; Jm 5:16) presenting to the Father 'the joy and hope, the grief and anguish of the men of our time, especially of those who are poor or afflicted in any way' (*Gaudium et Spes, 1*).

Tenderness turned into intercession

These basic clarifications regarding intercessions encourage a proper understanding of 'pray for us sinners'.

Mary's intercession in our favour with the Father of mercies and the God of expectations is always through Christ, with Christ and in Christ, the intercessor who cannot be substituted and with whom the Spirit has uniquely associated her, and it is always performed jointly with the Church, of which she is part and a holy figure.

It is precisely from a spiritual understanding of Mary as the all holy, that the Church at prayer sees in its own archetype, in its own exemplary figure, a powerful intercessory presence. It contemplates in Mary, as already in Elijah (Jm 5:17) and in line with the great intercessors of Israel, the fulfilment of the Scriptures both old and new: 'the eyes of the Lord are on the upright, his ear turned to their cry' (1Pt 3:12; Ps 33[34]:16).

The history of Western and Eastern Christian spirituality has confirmed and confirms that entrusting oneself to the maternal countenance and to the tender heart of the Woman who is able to make intercession, is an act to which the Spirit prompts every creature under the sun which finds itself in need. Those unable to accept the love of God and to love God and their neighbour, that is sinners, are not afraid to beg for forgiveness and for the Spirit when they are upheld by a cloud of intercessors, believers with Mary among them.

Our approach to the Father of generosity is made through the Son, in the Spirit and supported by the communion of the saints.

Among these, the eyes of our Advocate, full of tenderness, hold a particular place as we recall what she constantly performs: prayer for the salvation of us sinners.

NOW AND AT THE HOUR OF DEATH – AMEN

Today and the hour

Mary, she who is enlightened, knows 'how to pray properly' (Rm 8:26), asking for forgiveness and for the Spirit (Lk 11:13). The Spirit is the power of God who is able to transform the life of sinners, making them daily more and more 'moulded to the pattern of [the] Son' (Rm 8:29), both in life and in death.

Intercession goes to the roots of our human need, that is for forgiveness and for the Spirit, in order that we might become what we are called to be, icons of the Son. Increasingly set free from the idolatry of the 'I' so as to be completely amenable to God and his will, which is that we fill 'now' and 'the hour of our death' with a deeply evangelical sense, acting in all things, in life and in death, 'as he [the Lord] acted' (1 Jn 2:6).

It is a question of redeeming the present and of giving meaning to our passing days by 'doing good' (Ac 10:38) like Jesus, moved by a measureless love of the Father and of the whole of creation and prompted by a heart of friendship, overflowing with the Spirit of love whose fruit 'is love, joy, peace, patience, kindness, goodness, trustfulness, gentleness and self-control' (Ga 5:22).

It is a question of redeeming 'the hour of death' from its terrible meaninglessness and from its negative and unnatural aspect, in order to accept it and live it as the Lord Jesus did.

In trustful obedience even while experiencing extreme abandonment: 'Abba, Father!... For you everything is possible. Take this cup away from me. But let it be as you, not I, would have it' (Mk 14:36). '[At] the ninth hour Jesus cried out in a loud voice... "My God, my God, why have you forsaken me?" (Mk 15:34). 'Jesus cried out in a loud voice saying, "Father, into your hands I commit my spirit." With these words he breathed his last' (Lk 23:46).

In freedom: 'The Father loves me, because I lay down my life in order to take it up again. No one takes it from me; I lay it down of my own free will, and as I have power to lay it down, so I have power to take it up again; and this is the command I have received from my Father' (Jn 10:17-18).

In love: 'I have come so that they may have life and have it to the full. I am the good shepherd: the good shepherd lays down his life for his sheep' (Jn 10:10-11). 'No one can have greater love than to lay down his life for his friends' (Jn 15:13). 'So it is proof of God's own love for us, that Christ died for us while we were still sinners (Rm 5:8).

Just as birth, life and death are inseparable in the life of Christ, so are they also in that of the Christian, his icon.

Those born of the Spirit in Baptism are called to live in freedom and love and, in the same Spirit, to enter into death with the Lord, undertaking it as the event which crowns a life of *agape*. Losing our own life is not a more or less resigned acceptance of an event which is stronger than ourselves, but something offered to the Father that he might convert it into an occasion of blessing for all humanity and into a seed which might hasten the glorious coming of the Kingdom.

We can say with Paul: 'It makes me happy to be suffering for you now, and in my own body to make up all the hardships that still have to be undergone by Christ' (Col 1:24) in view of the new heavens and new earth, which are exemplified in him who is risen and transfigured and in her who is assumed into the realm of God.

Death is thus the crowning manifestation of the Christian vocation: to die to ourselves and to live no longer for ourselves but only for God and for his Kingdom of light which shines on everyone until their last breath, entrusting each with their own eternal destiny. In this lies the redemption of our own 'day' and our own 'hour'.

Amen

'Amen' concludes the second part of the *Hail Mary*. The root *m n* contains two definite meanings: to remain steadfast in someone and in his/her teaching of truth, prompted by a sure trust.

'Amen' is in fact the response of the believer to his own God, the God of the fathers and Father of Jesus Christ, and amounts to proclaiming, to our own conscience and publicly, that our life and our death find stability and meaning only in God and in his Word.

Isaiah 7:9 expresses this truth with the utmost conciseness and clarity: 'If you will not take your stand on me you will not stand firm'. Following in the same line of thought is Luke 6:47-48: 'Everyone who comes to me and listens to my words and acts on them – I will show you what such a person is like. Such a person is like the man who, when he built a house, dug, and dug deep, and laid the foundations on rock; when the river was in flood it bore down on that house but could not shake it, it was so well built.'

In the context of the *Hail Mary*, the 'Amen' expresses and evokes a deep desire which translates into prayer:

*O Virgin,
together with the just of Israel,
with the whole Church
of every place and all times,
in heaven and on earth,
in the company of the just
who have dwelt and dwell
in every continent,
receive our prayer.
In Christ
intercede for us
with the Father
that we may not lack
the good wine of the Spirit,
the divine power who,
by grafting us into the Son,
into the Father
and into their gospel of love,*

sets us firm as on a rock.
May it truly be so:
thus we hope and believe with trust,
aware that only he is our support.

CONCLUSION

'Rejoice, because God is truly with you as a loving presence who graces you, forgiving you and pouring out his Spirit upon you. Be joyful in this inexpressible blessing. The Spirit in you, like the dew which makes the desert bloom, makes you bearers of the Son into a world for which you must constantly make intercession.'

Mary, the purest image of the Church, stands in your midst as a reminder. Daily she recalls our attention that what matters is to become like her.

Becoming like her, perfect icon of the Son, means assuming each day more and more the form of Christ. This is the hidden vocation of every creature under the sun, in the expectation of being taken up, unveiled, into his Kingdom of peace.

Lectio divina of the *Hail Mary* produces its fruit in plenty only when we become aware that what is said of Mary is said to us.

THE STRUCTURE OF PERSONAL *LECTIO DIVINA*

In the course of this book, especially in the first part, we have said much about *lectio divina*. It is fitting to summarize our points and to set them down in a systematic way, properly completed, so as to offer the reader an outline of it not just as information (what is it) but also practically (how actually to perform it).

These notes only deal with personal *lectio divina*.

Preliminaries

Lectio divina is normally performed on the scriptural texts offered each day by the liturgy of the Church: on the Gospel or the first reading, or on both in its advanced exercise.

Similarly, *lectio* can be performed on a certain book of the Bible or on particular sections of Scripture: for example, the Beatitudes, the accounts of the Passion, the *Our Father* and the *Hail Mary*. Since the *Hail Mary* is a prayer which is in part literally scriptural and in part scripturally founded, it is also appropriate for *lectio divina*.

Why, as a norm, the biblical texts from the liturgy of the day? The reason is very simple and reflects the nature of the gift. No one may 'appropriate' holy Scripture to 'oneself' and no one may deal with it at pleasure. On the contrary, like the Eucharist, the ministries and charisms, it is a gift which the Father offers to his own, through the Son who is present in the Church. To receive with gratitude the daily portion of the Word given generously by the Father through the Church, is to proclaim the nature of the gift.

It is also to recognize the mercy and uprightness of a Father and a Church who have no personal preferences (Ac 10:34), but extend to all the same food, the source of life and unity.

It would be desirable, in order to underline the inherent characteristics of *lectio divina* as gift and something ecclesial, that the list of scriptural readings proposed for the week be distributed every Sunday at the end of the homily, accompanied by an exhortation by the priest or the bishop to feed on it as on daily bread. This would give rise to unimaginable developments.

It is further desirable that *lectio divina* take place early in the morning, in harmony with a tradition of listening which is already witnessed in Isaiah 50:4: 'Morning by morning he makes my ear alert to listen like a disciple.' The reason is twofold: so that the first Word heard be that of him who loves us as none other and so that it may be the first and only one to direct our daily journey and may make us able to weigh and consider the multitude of messages which bombard us during the day. May the Word of God present in the Scriptures be the ultimate criterion of our behaviour and judgement.

Certain things are necessary for *lectio divina*:

– a complete Bible,
– a daily missal,
– a readiness to give time to the
   God who speaks,

– a rethinking of your own house, apartment or room, now seen also as the location of your appointment with the Lord. 'Look, I am standing at the door, knocking. If one of you hears me calling and opens the door, I will come in...' (Rv 3:20).

Structure

1. The reading itself must be preceded by an *epiclesis,* or invocation of the Spirit, so that freed from all distractions the heart and the

mind might be directed exclusively to the scriptural text. This may be a free invocation or it may consist of the progressive recitation of a verse from the classical hymns to the Holy Spirit, such as the *Veni Creator* (Come Holy Ghost, Creator, come) and the *Veni Sanctae Spiritus* (Come, Holy Spirit).

2. After the *epiclesis* there follows the reading *(lectio)* of the text offered by the liturgy of the day. Not a hasty reading, lest the words slip away as water on stone, nor an incomplete reading, but one attentive to parallel references which the passage calls to mind or which are marked in the margin of the biblical page or in footnotes. Only from a global reading can one or more verses release the wealth of meaning which is hidden in them and never exhausted.

In fact, *lectio divina* is characterized as a reading of the Bible with the Bible; a reading perhaps repeated so that through what has been given it may be possible to understand even in its allusions what is being read.

3. After the reading there follows meditation *(meditatio)* or pondering of the passage. The message drawn from the text is held in the heart and reflected upon in the company of the Holy Spirit, who helps us to

understand it as the Word of God for us. A Word which consoles, corrects, guides, reproves and calls us to conversion of life. Meditation is the phase when the Word is interiorised or personalized.

It is the moment of determining the

4. Meditation is followed by contemplation *(contemplatio)* and prayer (*adoratio*). It is the adoring contemplation of a God who is really near to us – so near as to speak to us in the Son, Jesus Christ, hidden in every page of the Scripture, both the Old and New Testaments. Adoring and invoking contemplation of the Father and of the Word, and only of them, in the Spirit who, day after day, determine with their message our very existence. The adoring contemplation of a God with whom it intercedes so that through his own words everyone may discover the source of life and every community its inspiration to pray.

In this way, the presence that speaks through the book becomes the source of prayer.

5. After contemplation and prayer there follows action *(actio)*, praxis. The Word which is read *(oratio)*, meditated *(meditatio)*, contemplated *(contemplatio)* and

prayed *(adoratio)* sends us back into the arena of daily life so that it may be lived *(actio)*: 'you must do what the Word tells you and not just listen to it and deceive yourselves' (Jm 1:22).

The parable comes to an end. The Word and his message contained in Scripture flows into you, in order that in the midst of humanity you yourself might become Christ's living letter.

INDEX OF BIBLICAL REFERENCES

Old Testament

Genesis	
2:7	66
26:24	38
28:15	38

Exodus	
3:7,10-12	38
4:10-12	38
19:6	34, 61

Leviticus	
19:2	59, 61

Numbers	
23:19	59

Deuteronomy	
6:4	19
7:7	33, 40
7:8	33
8:17	33
9:4	33
28:4	53

Judges	
5:24	48
6:11-12,14-16	39

Psalms	
33(34):16	75
103(104):31	49
118(119):1-2,8	20
118(119):16,105	23

Isaiah	
6:3	59
7:9	80
50:4	86
50:4-5	20
55:8-9	59
55:9	22
61:10	27
63:10	45

Jeremiah	
1:4-8	39
2:7	34

Ezekiel	
16:8-14	34

Hosea	
2:21-22	35
11:1,3-4	34
11:9	59

Zephaniah	
3:14-17	25

Zechariah			Micah	
2:14	27	6:8		34
9:9	25		Judith	
9:9-10	25	13:8		48
Song of Songs			Joel	
4:7	28	2:21-27		25

New Testament

Matthew		1:34	21, 37, 39
2:1-12	57	1:35	28, 39, 58, 65
5:16	51, 52	1:37	40
5:44	73	1:38	41, 64
6:7	21	1:39-45	21
13:9	23	1:39-46	57
13:21	23	1:41-42,45	11, 29
13:22	23	1:42	9, 48, 53
13:23	23	1:43	65
Mark		1:45	22, 51
11:9	54	1:46-47	22, 27, 28
15:34	78	1:48	29, 40, 47, 53
14:36	78	1:49	11, 40, 47
		1:79	55
Luke		2:10-11	27
1:26-38	19	2:11	49, 55
1:27	64	2:19	21
1:28	9, 32, 35, 36, 40	2:30-32	40
1:28, 38	40	2:31-32	70
1:30-31	32	2:32	31, 49
1:31-32	64	2:35	22
1:32	28	2:48	21
1:32, 35	40	2:50	22

2:51	68
3:6	27, 49
3:22	54
6:27-28	55
6:28	73
6:35-36	56
6:47-48	20, 80
8:19-21	19
9:35	54
11:27-28	19
11:13	77
15:7,9-10, 23-24,32	27
18:19	60
23:34	72
23:46	78
24:36-52	27

John

1:1	65
1:14	36, 62, 65
2:1	65
2:5	21
3:16	43
5:14	73
5:44	52
10:10-11	23, 79
10:17-18	78
14:9	62
14:16-17	71
14:23-24	62
15:13	79
15:14-15	20
15:16	73
17:9,12,15	72
17:20-21	72
19:5	66
19:26-27	18

Acts

1:8	44
1:14	12, 15, 18, 44
2:33	54
2:42	55
3:6-7	44
3:14	58
3:25-26	54
4:12	55
4:32	55
6:8	31
8:30	16
10:4	14
10:34	85
10:38	77
26:16-18	55

Romans

3:24	15
5:8	79
8:26	77
8:29	77
8:34	72
10:1	14
15:30	14, 73

1 Corinthians

1:26-29	43
1:29	52
12:27	73

2 Corinthians

1:11	14
1:19	27
4:15	47
7:9-10	23
8:9	43

9:14	73, 74	2:1-2	73
13:7,9	73	6:16	59

Galatians

3:8-14	54
4:4	64
4:4-7	69
4:5	65
5:22	78

Ephesians

1:3	46, 54
1:4	36, 63
1:5	47
1:6-7	47
1:8	47
1:16	73
4:30	45
5:20	47
5:27	36
6:18	14, 74

Philippians

1:4,9	73
2:6-8	68

Colossians

1:3	73
1:12	47
1:16	66
1:24	79
3:15	47
4:3	14, 73
4:12	73

2 Thessalonians

3:1	14

1 Timothy

2:1	14

2 Timothy

1:3	73

Titus

2:11-14	35
2:13	36
2:14	36
3:1-8	36
3:3-9	35
3:5-6	36

Hebrews

7:25	15, 72

James

1:22	89
2:5	42
5:16	14, 15, 74
5:17	75

1 Peter

2:9	62
3:12	14, 75
3:9	56

1 John

2:1	15, 72
2:6	77
2:20,27	62
3:9	62

Revelation

3:20	86
4:8	59
5:12-13	54
8:4	14
21:3-4	45